Bra and Bathtub Fish

by Myka-Lynne Sokoloff
illustrated by Siri Weber Feeney

Harcourt
SCHOOL PUBLISHERS

Printed in Mexico

ISBN 10: 0-15-351551-1
ISBN 13: 978-0-15-351551-4

Ordering Options
ISBN 10: 0-15-351215-6 (Grade 5 Advanced Collection)
ISBN 13: 978-0-15-351215-5 (Grade 5 Advanced Collection)
ISBN 10: 015-358141-7 (package of 5)
ISBN 13: 978-0-15-358141-0 (package of 5)

1 2 3 4 5 6 7 8 9 10   126   12 11 10 09 08 07 06

Stacey stormed into the kitchen. "Mom! I need to go shopping, right now!" she demanded. "My science project is due on Friday, and I still need some supplies."

"Goodness, Stacey. You knew about this project weeks ago. Why have you waited until the last minute? My bread is due on Friday, too," Mrs. Levine joked, "and I can hardly drop what I'm doing this moment. Besides, I really hate going to the mall when it's full of holiday revelers."

Stacey's mother was making bread for Friday night's Sabbath dinner. The Jewish Sabbath—a day of rest—begins at sundown on Friday. Stacey's family celebrates it each week by eating bread called *challah* and lighting special candles.

Mrs. Levine's arms were plunged halfway up to her elbows in a bowl of bread dough. The dough was golden from egg yolks and as sticky as flypaper. Stacey watched as her mother scooped the gooey dough from the bowl with her fingers and dumped it onto a large wooden board.

Mrs. Levine sprinkled some flour over the surface of the board and then began to knead the dough. She pressed it with the heels of her hands, working in the dry flour as she turned the lump with rhythmic motions.

Stacey gazed hypnotically as the dough began to take the shape of a soft, round pillow. It looked irresistible. Stacey wanted to play with the smooth, elastic dough herself. "Can I help?" she asked.

"First scrub your hands with soap and then dry them thoroughly," her mother nodded.

Stacey followed her mother's instructions. Then she asked, "Why do you make challah from scratch, Mom? You don't have time with your job and raising *me*."

"It's just something I love to do. I find it relaxing, and it helps me remember my roots. I used to help my mother make challah each week when I was your age. My mother learned from her mother."

Nana's Challah

6 1/2 teaspoons dry yeast

2 teaspoons salt

4 eggs + extra yolk

6 tablespoons butter + hot water to equal 2 cups

7 cups flour

1/2 cup sugar

1. Mix yeast with salt, sugar, and 1 cup flour in large bowl.
2. Add water and butter to yeast mixture. Mix until well blended.
3. Stir in rest of flour.
4. Turn out onto floured board and knead 10 minutes.
5. Place in oiled bowl, cover, and place bowl in warm area for about an hour, until dough doubles in size.
6. Punch dough and knead briefly.
7. Divide into four parts. Divide each part in thirds.
8. Roll pieces to form ropes slightly longer than bread pan.
9. Braid 3 ropes together. Place in pan. Repeat with other loaves.
10. Paint top of loaves with egg yolk mixed with 1 teaspoon water. Sprinkle sesame or poppy seeds if desired.
11. Let loaves rise in warm area for about 45 minutes.
12. Bake at 375°F (191°C) for about 30 minutes.

"Tell me about when they were little," Stacey begged.

Mrs. Levine's voice became raspy, touched with emotion as she remembered her own mother and grandmother. She looked especially wistful as she recalled her beloved *bubbe*.

"My grandmother, Bubbe Golda, kept fish in the bathtub." Mrs. Levine recalled the story from the days when she would beg her mother to tell her stories from the past as they made challah together.

"No way!" shrieked Stacey. "Yuck! Who scrubbed the tub? Was it Nana?" Stacey wanted to know. "That must have been a grim job!"

Mrs. Levine nodded and continued. "Bubbe Golda insisted on using fresh whitefish or carp to make her *gefilte* fish for the Sabbath. She bought a live fish each week and let it swim in the bathtub until she was ready to cook it."

"The family lived in an apartment, so there was nowhere else to keep the fish. Each week, Bubbe Golda would clean a fish and use the meat to make *gefilte* fish, those little balls of fish that we eat with horseradish."

"I always thought *gefilte* fish came from a jar."

"Of course, that's how most people get it today, but people used to make it themselves each week."

"Well, I'm just glad we don't have fish swimming in our bathtub." Stacey made a face at the thought.

Mrs. Levine smiled. "Times have changed. My grandmother used to do all the work herself to get ready for the Sabbath. Now many people buy prepared foods, and sometimes you and your brother even pitch in. That makes my job considerably easier."

Mrs. Levine stopped to test the dough Stacey was kneading. She pressed it gently with a fingertip. It was just right, neither tough nor sticky, but silky and smooth.

"That's enough kneading now, I think," Mrs. Levine decided. "Go finish your homework while the dough rises."

When Stacey finished her work, she returned to the kitchen. "What's next?" she asked as her mother tested the puffy dough.

"Now I'll cut the dough into pieces to make separate loaves." She divided the dough, saving some to make small dinner rolls.

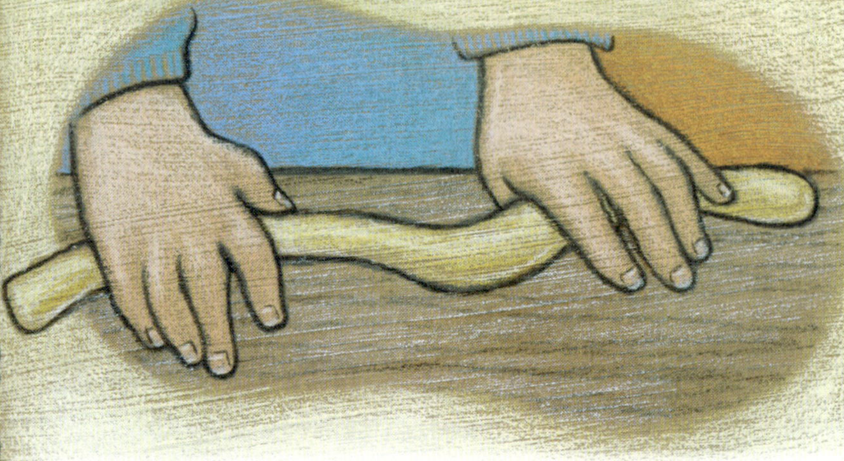

"Here's an easy math problem for you. We need to make four loaves. Each loaf, of course, is braided from three pieces. How many pieces do we need to cut?"

"Eleven," Stacey joked, just to make sure her mother was listening. "Come on, Mom, give me a harder question."

Stacey followed the motions her mother demonstrated, twisting the three strands of dough together. "This isn't as hard as it looks. It's just like braiding my hair. Why does the challah have a braid with three parts?" she asked.

"Well," Mrs. Levine replied thoughtfully, "I like to think of it as the past, present, and future braided together. Making it is a tradition I learned from my mother. She learned it from her mother. Now I'm passing it on to you."

"Do you think Nana ever got into trouble when she was a girl?" Stacey wondered as her hands neatly crisscrossed strands of dough. "She always seems so proper and, well, perfect now."

"Well, I doubt that she ever stormed around in a bad mood like you do sometimes," her mother said with a wink. "I do remember hearing a funny story about something naughty she did once, though."

"What happened?" Stacey asked.

"I know of only one time she misbehaved," her mother responded. "I guess she did it out of love.

"Bubbe Golda was planting her vegetable garden. This was when they lived in the old country, before they moved to America and lived in an apartment. She was planting rows of little tomato plants. It was hot working in the sun, and clouds of mosquitoes swarmed around her."

"What happened?" Stacey repeated, more intently.

"Nana was about your age. The family had little money and many children. Bubbe Golda worked from morning until night taking care of her family. She helped out in her husband's business as well. Nana got to thinking that her mother looked tired all the time. She wanted to do something that would make less work for Bubbe Golda."

"What did she do?" Stacey urged her mother to complete the tale.

"As soon as Bubbe Golda finished planting all those tomatoes and went indoors, Nana went right behind her and pulled each plant out of the ground! She threw them into the creek that ran by the house."

"No! Why would she do something so destructive?" Stacey wondered in horror. "Did she get in trouble?"

"Nana thought she would save Bubbe Golda work by pulling out the seedlings. No weeding. No watering. She didn't think about the fact that there would be no tomatoes either," Mrs. Levine chuckled. "I don't think Nana got punished because when she saw how upset Bubbe Golda was, she confessed what she had done. Bubbe Golda realized that she was only trying to help. Together they planted more tomato plants. Children don't always realize when they are making more work for their parents," she added.

"I'll clean up from our baking, and I'll wash the pans later on, Mom," Stacey said, taking the hint. She was feeling a bit guilty about dragging her mother to the store for her science project.

"I'm always happy to have your help, Sweetie," Mrs. Levine continued. "I'm grateful, too, that you are interested in hearing about your family history. The past is a foundation for the future, you know."

"Now," Mrs. Levine said, wiping her hands on her apron and piling bowls and boards into the sink, "why don't we wash up together? Then we can go to the store and get what you need for your project. When we come home, the bread should be ready for the oven."

"I can't wait until the challah is baked. That smell is always appealing. Can I have some of the rolls tonight?" Stacey urged.

"You earned it, Stacey. I completed my chores with your help. Now let's go take care of you."

Stacey thought about Nana's story while she washed up.

"Uh, Mom," she said. "You don't need to take me to the store anymore. You gave me lots of good ideas for my project, and I don't want to make any extra work for you. I've decided to do my project on what makes dough rise. I've got everything I need right here at home."

Think Critically

1. How does this story connect to the theme of common goals?

2. Describe three different settings that are included in the story.

3. What did you find surprising about this story? Explain your answer.

4. Does Stacey remind you of a character from another story you have read? In what way?

5. What did Stacey learn from the story her mother told about Nana?

 Social Studies

Food Customs Use the Internet or some cookbooks to find recipes for breads from different countries. Make a recipe book. Ilustrate the book.

School-Home Connection Tell your family about this book. Then talk about a project that you could do together. You may wish to cook something together like Stacey and her mother did. Discuss ways that each family member could contribute.

Word Count: 1,558